The and Your Church

Reaching Out to Those
Who Struggle

John Freeman

New
Growth
Press
www.newgrowthpress.com

New Growth Press, Greensboro, NC 27404
www.newgrowthpress.com
Copyright © 2013 by World Reformed Fellowship

All Scripture quotations, unless otherwise indicated are from *The Holy Bible, English Standard Version*® (ESV®), copyright © 2000, 2001 by Crossway Bibles, a division of Good News Publishers. Used by permission. All rights reserved.

Scripture quotations marked NIV are taken from the *Holy Bible, New International Version*®, NIV®. Copyright © 1973, 1978, 1984, 2011 by Biblica, Inc. Used by permission. All rights reserved worldwide.

Cover Design: Faceout books, faceout.com
Typesetting: Lisa Parnell, lparnell.com

ISBN-10: 1-939946-21-2
ISBN-13: 978-1-939946-21-8

Library of Congress Cataloging-in-Publication Data
Freeman, John, 1953–
 The gay dilemma and your church : reaching out to those who struggle / author John Freeman.
     pages cm
 Includes bibliographical references and index.
 ISBN 978-1-939946-21-8 (alk. paper)
 1. Homosexuality—Religious aspects—Christianity. 2. Church work with gays. I. Title.
 BR115.H6F74 2013
 277.3'08308664—dc23   2013020701

Printed in Canada

21 20 19 18 17 16 15 14   2 3 4 5 6

"I don't care—let them all go to hell." I had been explaining to a church leader the essence of our ministry and how we help people who contact us. His verbal response startled me, to say the least. The anger and vehemence in his statement took me aback.

A conversation with another church leader—this time about whether Christians could be gay and adopt both that label and identity—produced another response that startled me. He looked directly at me and said unwaveringly, "Gay Christians? What's wrong with Christians being gay?" It was not a question; it was a comment.

Like it or not, the church can no longer avoid responding to homosexuality. Almost everyone today knows someone who is gay or lesbian or otherwise impacted by homosexuality. In a real sense, homosexuality has embraced the culture, and the culture (and some churches) has embraced homosexuality. This makes a growing dilemma for many in the Christian community who are personally impacted by these issues, however much we might like to pretend otherwise.

The two leaders above represent two polarized responses toward homosexuality within the Christian community. Are our only two options to either turn our backs on homosexuals or embrace their lifestyle? How should God's people, his church, respond to those who struggle with homosexuality in our churches? How should we respond to those who have embraced homosexuality as a lifestyle? Like all areas of life, the Bible and the gospel of Jesus Christ have much to say about homosexuality. The gospel points us to a better response than either rejection or wholesale acceptance. There is God's way of mercy and truth for those who struggle with same-sex attraction (SSA) and for those who would seek to reach out to them.

Part of the Problem or Part of the Solution?

Most people reading this would probably agree that homosexual practice is wrong—that is, sinful. God's Word condemns homosexuality as a practice of heart, mind, and body in every place and in all instances. In fact, the Bible condemns all sexual acts outside what God institutes in Genesis 1:27–28, where the pattern for biblical sexual expression is defined in the context of marriage of one man and one woman. However, if we stop at just labeling homosexuality as sinful, we fall far short of presenting a redemptive and Christlike response to a growing dilemma for the household of faith. Many of us are dealing with these deeply heart-wrenching struggles in our own lives and in the lives of those we love.

As Christians we must take responsibility for some of the theological and ideological "mess" in which we find ourselves. Historically, we've either ignored this major human dilemma for many people, or we've separated or detached it from other types of sexual sin. We've expected some type of magical, spontaneous resolution about serious questions of identity and sin issues to emerge from afar, rather than encouraging our people to be honest about these embarrassing, shame-ridden, and very real problems. We haven't assigned the issues the same significance God has—that this is, and always has been, part of the fallen order of things—even though we often think we have. Truly, nothing is new under the sun, although we've mistakenly let our people think, "Surely none of us would struggle with *that*."

That hands-off mentality by the church over the last fifty years has contributed to the gay communities of our country becoming one of the fastest growing "people groups" in history. Many in the gay community now find friendship, support, encouragement, solace, and real community among their own. They take comfort in others who understand their struggles and plight, their past rocky and painful road to self-acceptance, as well as their current stresses—often with extended family and the church.

Additionally, we've made it hard for anyone in the church to admit that they are struggling with SSA and homosexuality by relegating this particular sin struggle to a category of "other." By treating SSA as different from and set apart from other sexual struggles and sin, we have made it difficult for those who struggle and their friends to bring the light of God's love and mercy into this struggle. Due to its nature, we've assigned it to that dark corner of the room where the light cannot shine.

Years ago, my mission seminary professor, Harvie Conn, taught on 1 Corinthians 6:9–10: "Or do you not know that the unrighteous will not inherit the kingdom of God? Do not be deceived: neither the sexually immoral, nor idolaters, nor adulterers, nor men who practice homosexuality, nor thieves, nor the greedy, nor drunkards, nor revilers, nor swindlers will inherit the kingdom of God." He stressed the fact that living an unrepentant life regarding these things was something that could get you in much trouble, in this life and the next. But he also stressed that this passage taught that there are consequences for heterosexual sinners as there are for homosexuals, as well as for those who commit more "acceptable," non-sexual sins.

I learned from him (and from the Bible!) that we need to take *all* sin seriously, not just those we find personally offensive or distasteful, or those we can't identify with or see ourselves committing. All sin is an offense to God, whatever its nature, sexual or otherwise.

Same-sex attractions are usually first felt and experienced at an early age by youth who don't ask for them and who didn't go around saying to themselves "I think I'll be gay when I grow up." By placing same-sex attractions outside the realm of other "normal" sexual sin struggles, we've created a silent space that has fostered neglect, pastorally speaking. The culture, our own fallen hearts, and the strategies of the evil one have conspired to confuse, confound, and shipwreck our faith and has led many of us to fail to understand and respond as Scripture commands us. Of this neglect, we must repent. We are now reaping the fruit of many years of not discussing and addressing these things, pastorally and proactively, at all levels of church life.

Does this mean we turn the other way and ignore sin and disobedience? Absolutely not. It *does* mean that the motive of our own hearts in addressing this sin must be one of genuine love and compassion— as Christ responds to others in the Scripture who are caught in sins of a sexual nature. Any kind of response by God's people must be redemptive in nature. We need to realize that those who struggle with and are captured by sexual sin are always among the broken-hearted. Whether recognized or admitted, emptiness and despair are the companions of not only homosexuality, but all sin.

What are we, the church, doing to reach, share the gospel with, and rescue those who deal with same-sex attractions and homosexuality? What might that look like?

Any efforts along these lines must be intentional.

It requires a plan, a focus, and a strategy, just as it would to try to reach anyone caught in life-dominating problems. We can no longer negate or deny the fact that our people are increasingly bringing a multitude of scars and open wounds regarding sex and sexuality into their relationship with Christ. Also, what is generally happening and being experienced by people "out there" is also impacting folks in the pew. No one escapes falling for the false appeal of sin.

Of course, the primary place to begin is in our own congregations. Intentionality in this area means proactively educating our youth. It's in the early years, usually around age ten today, when many of our youth first wrestle with these things. Admittedly, twenty-five years ago most youth weren't asking at age ten, "Am I gay?" Today they *are* asking that question, earlier and earlier. Biased and agenda-driven vehicles of the culture that we cannot effectively escape—movies, television, the media, music, and the secular education system—force the question onto our youth all too soon.

We must equip and involve all those in youth ministry, starting in early middle-school ministry—including Sunday school teachers, volunteer leaders, and especially youth staff—about these issues. We want twelve-year-old Jimmy to be able to approach a trusted male in our youth ministry and admit, "I'm looking at pictures I shouldn't be on the computer and I know it's wrong." We want fourteen-year-old Suzy to be able to go to a trusted woman in our church and confess, "I think I'm a lesbian. What do I do now?" Unfortunately, it's been my experience that most youth workers are woefully unprepared, and often left stunned and speechless at such revelations. Any youth worker or youth pastor not able and willing to address these issues head-on, regularly and compassionately, should not be in youth ministry today!

If more of our churches were equipped to handle these real heart questions, we might not see so many of our churched youth gravitating toward and influenced by gay and lesbian student unions and homosexual organizations on the high school and college campus. We might not see so many of our youth genuinely seeking help for their questions and struggles from the Internet—only to be further taken in by falsehoods and bad theology concerning homosexuality. The "silent years"—when no preteen or teen talks about what's going on inside—must be intentionally addressed over and over again by our youth workers, along with varied and multiple permission-giving messages for disclosure. The church much be seen as a helpful and safe place for youth to disclose these struggles.

We also want our churches to offer concrete, pastoral help to adults struggling with homosexuality. Many men and women sit silently in our pews weighed down by the shame, guilt, and embarrassment of either ongoing same-sex attractions or a homosexual past that still impedes their personal relationships and their growth in Christ. Here again, repeated upfront, permission-giving messages need to be supplied from the leadership in all capacities, effectively communicating that "we know and expect that these struggles might be part of your experience—and we want to help. Together, we can handle this." Much too often contrary messages are given, both verbally and nonverbally, that convey "We're fragile in this area; we can't handle it." This must cease if we expect our people to voluntarily seek help. We must expect the gospel to do its work.

Being spiritually mature in our leadership means the end of naïveté.

This means admitting again the gravity of the fall and realizing that everything is *not* as it should be—including and especially, the sexual struggles of our people. Mature ministry takes people right where they are—in various states of delusion and sin. Consider these stunning words by a megachurch pastor:

> Every effective church will have sexual strugglers as well as others dealing with many other life-dominating sins in it. When these people sit in our

pews, they are all in various stages of dealing with their problems. Some are in denial that there is a problem. Some know their sin is against God's law and live lives of hypocrisy and deception. Some are struggling with various degrees of success and failure to make the changes God requires. Others are regularly and effectively accessing the grace present in the Gospel in order to live changed lives. The challenge of the church is to assist sinners at all of these stages. We flush out the self-deceived, expose the dishonest, confront the rebel, offer forgiveness to the guilt-crushed, provide hope to the despairing, and support the surrendered. In addition, the church must invite in and hold the attention of those who formerly would never dare look to the church for hope or help.[1]

We must proactively organize to help those who are struggling. Today, many churches successfully run Bible study/support groups or sexual integrity groups focused on these issues and problems for their members and the community. These are places where men and women can begin to address, often for the first time, what has fueled their hearts and led them into ungodly sexual lifestyles. They can also learn, with the help of other caring and supportive people, to address ways in which they are still tempted to walk in unbelief—the lies they tend to believe about others and their own identity, their false "functional" theology, and the faulty thinking by which they live.

It's also the place where people learn how to repent well. As one pastor put it, we must learn how to "kill that which is killing me, without killing myself." No one can do this on their own; it comes with assistance from the community of believers—including lay members of the congregation and perhaps those who have a special heart for people struggling with these specific "besetting" sins.

Any kind of intentional outreach must be based in both truth and mercy.

The foundation of mercy and truth is, of course, necessary for ministering to those within the church, but is much more crucial for those outside the church. I'm thinking here of those who are unbelievers, as well as those who may be regenerate but in open rebellion and those with deep scars and broken experiences with the church and "organized" Christianity. This too represents more people than ever today.

How do we minister to those not of the household of faith, or to those disillusioned, abandoned, and outside the church family? It still means that we minister to people with both the truth and mercy of the gospel. We don't water down God's revealed will about the illegitimacy of any type of sex out of bounds, including homosexuality. But we also do something that is most excellently mirrored and modeled through the incarnation: we willingly and joyfully jump into the trenches with others, in this case those pursuing or emerging from a gay identity or life.

Isn't that what Jesus did in leaving the riches of heaven and coming to earth for *us*? He left the most intimate, uninterrupted relationship there ever was to taste and experience the mud, muck, and mire of humanity. Gospel ministry to those in trouble sexually will do the same. Jesus did this for us; how can we not do it for others, especially in areas where the church has previously had a hands-off and uninvolved mentality?

Seeing a Person, Rather Than an Issue

Showing mercy to and sharing the gospel with those involved (either actively or passively) in homosexuality will look different in different circumstances. I believe, however, that effective biblical methods include some crucial elements. Obviously, we need to be saddened and grieved at the fact that anyone would see homosexuality as the solution to life's confusion and hurts. Let me be blunt: we need to be brought to tears, not only at ill-conceived ideas of where life may be found, but also at those *in outright rebellion*. Why is it that many believers respond to homosexuals with anger and disgust? Is that truly Christlike?

In Luke 19:41, Jesus was brought to tears and "wept over" Jerusalem—over those who hated him, mistreated him, rejected the truth, had specific agendas regarding him, and would ultimately take his life. We must ask God to give us his heart for the sexually broken and shattered. Even if they don't see themselves that way, *we* surely must, and we must be moved to reach out with compassion.

Today most of our culture's views and perceptions

of Christianity, especially as it relates to homosexuality, come from the ranting and ravings of television evangelists decrying the evils of homosexuality and of gays and lesbians defending themselves. Additionally, discussions of the legitimacy of homosexuality are often mixed and intertwined with the goals of political parties. In other words, the gospel and politics get mixed, resulting in a distorted view of Christianity. It can't be denied that this impacts the understanding and reception of the gospel.

David Kinnaman and Gabe Lyons's book *unChristian* states that ninety-one percent of those surveyed between the ages of sixteen and twenty-nine say Christianity is "anti-homosexual." Respondents claimed that Christians show excessive anger, disgust, and generally unloving attitudes toward homosexuals.[2] Clearly, the church is working from a public relations deficit and distortion. For most people, Christians have nothing of value to say about this topic. We must work at overcoming and addressing these deficits, the places the gospel has not been accurately proclaimed in the marketplace. It's up to us to change that paradigm. Yes, we will admit that sin is serious and destructive, but also share the gospel and increasingly talk about God's good gift of sex and sexuality, even as we weep over and with people.

We need to see homosexuals as Christ would—as *people*, not as an *issue*. When we reduce people to their sins or rebellion, we often react out of a deep motivation to set things right because our own sensibilities are offended. Sadly, I see this throughout the church

13

today. I've been involved in many discussions with congregations about this issue where it becomes clear that most people's (often unconscious) desire is for the homosexual to "just stop it," be like them, and become heterosexual—*not* to know Christ. Such a mind-set betrays our own fallen hearts and misguided unbiblical thinking.

Dealing with people as persons means that we see *them*—not the problem we want to fix or see changed. To do that, we must know who they are. Admittedly, getting to know people takes time and effort. But prayer, patience, and forbearance must be at the heart of any attempt to reach lost, hurting, confused, or disordered hearts of any kind! Our goal should not be that people are "set straight," but that they are won to Christ, either initially or in a deeper way—that they become true worshipers of the true God.

When believers proclaim the gospel to gays and to the culture at large in a loving, redemptive manner, punctuated with grace and truth, it sets us apart and truly reflects the person of Christ. In such a heated and emotional debate, Christians have a responsibility to represent Christ to a fallen world and those in homosexuality in four specific and distinct ways.

1. Patiently listen. "Everyone should be quick to listen, slow to speak" (James 1:19 NIV). We should not be looking for loopholes in a debate or seeking a chance to criticize, shame, or find fault, nor should we be looking for the next thing to say to defend our position. We listen to understand the "heart thrust" of what the other person is saying. This is hard work. It is not natural. It takes practice. Learning how to patiently listen is a way we love people with Christ's love.

Loving biblically means we take time to observe, to see the world through the other person's eyes and experience. When we speak too quickly to force our views or to point out error, we don't "see" the person, just the problem we think needs to be corrected. We often respond to that which makes us feel uncomfortable. The gospel, however, takes a deeper foothold when we enter the other person's world. We learn why people believe what they believe, what makes them who they are, what (or who) has hurt them in the past, and all that has hampered their "hearing." Treating people with respect, as image-bearers of God, helps deconstruct barriers.

Wasn't this Jesus's routine method of ministry? He dialogues with and engages the woman at the well—who may have been thinking he might just be the next better meal ticket (John 4:1–42). He compassionately, yet with spiritual authority, addresses the woman taken in adultery (John 8:1–11). He treats the sinful woman who pours perfume on his feet with respect (Mark 14:3–9). And for this, he was always being criticized for eating with and fellowshipping with "tax collectors and sinners" (Matthew 9:9–13).

In loving by listening, we learn much more about people and discover why they have sought after other false gods. When we don't take time to get to know people, we tend to lump them into groups, label them on the basis of what we read in the news about "those" people, and mistakenly think that we understand them.

2. Personally repent. "'Do you think that these Galileans were worse sinners than all the other Galileans? . . . No, I tell you; but unless you repent, you will all likewise perish'" (Luke 13:2–3). Only a redeemed sinner, knowing he stands condemned apart from Christ's death on a cross, can reach a sinner who doesn't know he needs redeeming. Therefore, check your motivation before you engage someone. Are you doing it to reach a lost person with the enduring love that has found you—a love that has exposed you as a cutthroat, a would-be fraud, and a depraved sinner who has been, through no merit of your own, embraced by fatherly love? Are you doing it out of the awareness that at heart you're a sham, a misfit, a counterfeit, a phony, and there is nothing good inside you to warrant God's love toward you? Do you really care about homosexuals as men and women who desperately need to know the love of the Father—or would you rather they all just shut up and disappear?

Remember Jesus's words: "He who is forgiven little, loves little" (Luke 7:47)—or, stated the opposite way, "He who has been forgiven much, loves much." How we treat other sinners shows how aware we are of our own continuous need for the gospel and the work of Christ in our lives. If we have no love for gays or lesbians, then we have not understood the forgiving love of Jesus in our own lives.

Where do we need to repent of our own bias and fears, of our noncaring and hard hearts? What log is in our own eye that must be removed before we, in humility, can confront or challenge others? Where do *we* need the gospel? What temptations or sinful habits do we continually need to be saved from? Ongoing awareness of our own temptations and besetting sins—and marveling in the fact that our own record has been expunged through the work of the cross—must give us a heart of repentance ourselves.

3. Gently instruct. "And the Lord's servant must not be quarrelsome but kind to everyone, able to teach, patiently enduring evil, correcting his opponents with gentleness. God may perhaps grant them repentance leading to a knowledge of the truth" (2 Timothy 2:24–25). How do we talk with people who don't believe what we believe? An argumentative, win-at-all-costs approach does not conform to what Paul wrote Timothy. We must ask the Holy Spirit to instruct our own hearts as we seek to instruct others. Having a gentle manner does not mean becoming weak or vacillating in our own arguments; it means treating everyone with dignity and respect, even when they persistently disagree or are hostile. In fact, we need to *expect* hostility. Harvest USA staff member Dave White writes:

> When you interact with someone entrenched in sin, realize they will often be prickly and cantankerous. In pointing them to God away from their idols, you are taking from them the very thing they are hoping for or seeking "life" in. When you call someone to abandon his false hopes, it feels like you are stealing his canteen of water and leaving him stranded in a desert. In their fear, loneliness, and despair they are prone to

lash out at those now offering a new source of life. The way you respond to these attacks is critical for the gospel to take root.[3]

I have been involved in many conversations with gays and lesbians, as well as with those who are sympathetic to gay causes. I've learned that it's okay to let people beat up on me verbally. I've learned that after an episode of someone being in my face for calling into question a deeply felt belief, there is usually a silent moment—a breathing space—that I can speak into with gentleness. It's then that I can often form a question aimed at the heart that is based on something the person has said.

Bearing with people in gentleness gives an open door to the gospel that neither retreating nor using a like-mannered heated response ever will! This disarms and opens up hearts like nothing else can. The problem is that our own fear, unbelief, anger, defensiveness, self-righteousness, and unpreparedness often gets in the way so that we never get to that point.

Talking to those who are blind to the reality of their hearts and who live in a world that supports and applauds spiritual rebellion is both a privilege and a challenge. They are victims of their own sin, as well as caught in the lies and sins of others. But they are also accountable before a holy God for their continued choices to live on their own terms and for their refusal to submit to Christ. We must address both of these realities as we share Christ.

Gently instructing also means being grounded in the Scripture, not our own opinions. The real issue regarding what Scripture says about homosexuality is not about whether key passages are culturally relevant anymore, but whether Scripture, in its entirety, still has authority over all life. It should always be the truths of Scripture, and not our demeanor or presentation of it, that people reject.

4. Mercifully pursue and then engage the heart. "And have mercy on those who doubt; save others by snatching them out of the fire; to others show mercy with fear, hating even the garment stained by the flesh" (Jude 22–23). God calls us to be neither reclusive nor rude, but to move boldly into confusing, high-stakes situations with the gospel of his mercy. This means we bring the gospel where it is most needed. We pursue and engage the vocally anti-Christian, pro-gay activist, the mild-mannered clergy who says the love of Jesus means affirming homosexuality as God's gift, the out-and-proud lesbian in our office, the confused and scared teenager who fears he's gay and believes there is no other option to pursue, and the sexually abused woman who now sees a relationship with a woman as her only hope.

Showing mercy means practically caring for people in spite of their confusion, fears, doubts, and fallen thinking. It means being patient and persistent and holding our ground with those who say we are hateful bigots because we disagree with their beliefs. As we do this we are enabled to move into other people's worlds intentionally and with genuineness and authenticity, as servants and fellow sinners.

Following Christ by Engaging People

I once approached a man who was marching in a gay rally for two hours in pouring-down rain in South Florida's ninety-eight-degree heat and humidity. I said, "Sir, may I speak with you for a moment?" (He paused.) "What's so important to you that you would spend two hours walking around in this heat and downpour? What point are you trying to get across here?" (The best kind of evangelism always begins with addressing the obvious—what's right in sight, what we hear and observe.)

Subsequently, we had a two-hour conversation that ended with him shaking my hand and thanking me for stopping him, in spite of the fact that I shared the gospel and asked him to consider if God might have a different plan for his life. I listened to him, heard his concerns, and then engaged his heart with matters important to him—and to God. He actually invited me to a party with the other demonstrators being held afterward.

Engaging people on this level gets them into their story more quickly than anything else, and that's what we want. When people get into their stories, their personal histories and experiences, they become more open to us and to the gospel. Jesus was the master of this and we should try to be like the Master. His methods are often the most underutilized aspects of evangelism, and yet they make the deepest and most heartfelt impact, often leaving people wanting more!

You may be thinking, *Okay, this is all fine and good, but where do faith and repentance come in?* My answer is "Everywhere!" Awareness of truth and conviction of sin come in many small steps before it becomes faith with a capital "F" and repentance with a capital "R." Jesus pursues us in many ways, in the context of both little and big things. He pursues us in traumas, problems, life's hurts and disappointments, the loss of friendships or jobs—even in life's successes, especially when we think we have it all and are happy, but then realize we're not. God uses all that life brings our way—especially when it crashes around us—to get our attention and cause us to begin to question decisions and choices. He uses all these same elements in the lives of homosexuals to bring them to Christ as well.

However, God rarely does this in a void. He uses other people—*his* people. I've seen this repeatedly in the lives of those who come to our ministry, or in any church-based ministry that helps those with out-of-control sexual desires and behaviors. In fact, that's the basis of one of Harvest USA's books, *Gay . . . Such Were Some of Us: Stories of Transformation and Change.*[4] The twelve stories in that book all testify to the power of others who were part of the process of faith and repentance in each life.

The homosexual sinner needs and must experience what we all must experience, what Thomas Chalmers called, "The Expulsive Power of a New Affection." He explains how our sin, our habits, and our flaws never just disappear by a process of reason or mental determination (understanding them or trying harder). But the bad affections of the heart—that by which we stand condemned, that which drives us into the dark places, that which corrupts, and that which robs us of true life—may be dispossessed by something greater.[5]

Only when we are truly melted and moved by the sight, knowledge, and sense of God in Christ will our natural affections be changed. Only when we begin to understand God's love for us in Christ through the riches of his grace will the appeal of our sin begin to pale in comparison. Only when grace is understood, applied, and lived out to the point that we realize we "stand" in grace because of Jesus—we don't crawl, creep, shuffle, or slink into it—then and only then will we see the deadly and life-robbing nature of idols of the heart. These same truths are true for those struggling with homosexuality.

A Puritan prayer so rightly captures the essence of this, of what has to happen in every heart, gay or straight: "When thy Son, Jesus, came into my soul instead of sin he became more dear to me than sin had formerly been; His kindly rule replaced sin's tyranny. Teach me to believe that if ever I would have any sin subdued I must not only labour to overcome it, but must invite Christ to abide in the place of it, and he must become more to me than that vile lust has been; that his sweetness, power, life may be there."[6]

Those caught in, but fighting, improper desires of homosexuality and those who have fully embraced homosexuality as a life and identity need the same thing and are changed by the very same truths. Do we have faith that this can happen? Do we believe the gospel still brings sight to the blind and releases prisoners? Are we willing to be part of this salvage-and-rescue effort for the glory of Christ and the reclamation of sinners?

If we agree that we must be about this saving work, it will radically change how we "do church," how we begin to boldly address these problem areas among our own people, and how we enter into and engage a lost and broken world.

Endnotes

1. "When Homosexuality Comes to Church," *Harvest News* (Summer 1992):1.

2. David Kinnaman and Gabe Lyons, *unChristian: What a New Generation Really Thinks about Christianity . . . and Why It Matters* (Grand Rapids, MI: Baker Books, 2007).

3. David White, "Developing Christ's Heart for the Brokenhearted," *Harvest News* (Fall 2004):2.

4. David Longacre, ed., *Gay . . . Such Were Some of Us: Stories of Transformation and Change* (Boone, NC: Upside Down Ministries, 2009).

5. Thomas Chalmers, "The Expulsive Power of a New Affection," http://manna.mycpanel.princeton.edu/resources/doc/158/raw (last accessed 1/25/13).

6. "Contentment," *The Valley of Vision: A Collection of Puritan Prayers and Devotion*, Arthur Bennett, ed. (Carlisle, PA: Banner of Truth, 2003), 163.